I0163765

Life, Love & Passion
Reflections of My Soul

Jamie Laster

DISCLAIMER: This book is a work of fiction. Names, characters, places, and incidents are the product of the authors' imaginations and/or are used fictitiously. Any resemblance to actual persons, living or dead, or to actual events or locations is pure coincidence.

Life, Love & Passion (1st Edition)

COPYRIGHT © 2014 by Jamie Laster & Jamie Ervin

Web Site
JamieLasterAuthor.com

ISBN (paperback): 978-1-939229-03-8
ISBN (ebook): 978-1-939229-02-1

Library of Congress Control Number
2014933563

Published by Flying Donkey Press – Placerville, CA
FlyingDonkeyPress.com

All Rights Reserved

Dedication

For my sons, Geramie and Jordan – for their unconditional love,
and being the reasons to never give up, to follow my dreams,
and to live by example.

To my mom, Alice O., and my sisters Joan, Barbara, and Corlis – for
all their love, support, and encouragement
as long as I can remember.

To the Caveman – for helping to re-energize my creative spirit.

To the rest of my family and friends for all your encouragement and
support of my writing- especially finishing this first book – a
tremendous thank you … I love you all.

Contents

Mama's Bed

When I was a little girl and I was sad,
I loved to climb into my Mama's bed.
Even though she wasn't in the room.
I felt her presence.
I could just lay there,
think it all out,
and get grounded once again.
In Mama's bed all my problems seemed smaller.
In Mama's bed,
my soul was soothed.
In Mama's bed,
there was no concept of time.
Pillows smelling slightly of lavender,
I would stack them up,
and pull the covers up high around my neck.
I was transported to another place.
Calming, comforting, cathartic.
If I fell asleep, Mama never woke me up - she always let me
sleep.
Mama's bed worked its magic during my slumber.
Yesterday I found my youngest son asleep in *my* bed,
I left the room and closed the door.

Tick Tock

No amount of wishing or hoping, can bring back yesterday.
Here once and forever gone.
Unfinished business, unattained goals, unspoken words,
remain just that -
unfinished, unattained and unspoken.
Too many lost yesterdays will weigh you down.
Wallowing in the wasteland of *if onlys* changes nothing.
The past has already happened.
Maybe tomorrow will come, maybe it will not.
Those tomorrows cannot be counted upon - they are not
guaranteed.
It is today that we must laugh.
It is today that we must live.
It is easy to forget to love,
It is easy to forget to embrace time -
time which will inevitably slip away.
Seconds to minutes, minutes to hours
Tick tock, tick tock.
Time can be your friend, time can be your enemy.
It is today we that we must bask in the sun.
Chase the sun - even on the rainiest of days.

Super Mom

I am not tired from this morning's frantic rush,
of getting the boys up, dressed, fed,
and dropped off at before school daycare.
I just couldn't be tired after dealing with all the traffic delays,
in sluggish, snail speed commuter traffic
on the way to work ...
all the while knowing in less than nine hours
that I will have to repeat the frenetic race,
so I can pick the boys up from after school daycare on time.
Stopped at the grocery store and almost made it home -
until reminded of a project due tomorrow.
A project I wasn't told about in the first place,
so no choice but to head back to Michaels for art supplies.
There is just no way that I can possibly be tired
after cooking dinner, washing dishes, supervising homework,
giving baths,
then finally reading bedtime stories to each of the boys.
I am a mom after all, so I do have super powers ... *don't I* ?
As I reach over to stop the incessant,
beep, beep, beep of my alarm clock,
I can hear the muted murmur from the television,
advising me of today's weather and news of an upcoming
sale at Macy's.
Squinting from the harsh, unfriendly light of the ceiling fan,
I slowly realize that I am lying on top of the covers on my
bed.
The television has been on all night again.
Am still fully clothed from yesterday, one shoe on,
eyeglasses still intact and on my face.
Well .... certainly didn't happen because I was tired.

Reach for It

Sometimes you have to find someone
or something
to be that strong hand
you can reach out and grab -
to help pull you out of the quicksand
before you are completely engulfed.
You cannot harmoniously co-exist,
with feelings of guilt, shame or unworthiness.
They will weigh down your heart
dragging you to dwell,
deep in the dark, depressing , depths of despair.
Sometimes it is very difficult to live - really live,
and embrace all the gifts given to us.
Deep breath in,
exhale hard.
Deeper breath in,
exhale harder.
Life may be what you make it,
but at times
it may feel impossible to even get out of bed.
Curled tight in a ball,
barely able to focus on the floor
where you want to be standing.
Your legs just won't move.
Overwhelmed.
Overwrought.
Overstrung.
The phone ringing,
the doorbell chiming,
can't seem to break the spell.
Deep breath in,
exhale hard.
Deeper breath in,

exhale harder.
Life is full of changes,
and sometimes brings events
that can turn your world
upside down and inside out.
But it's never too late,
to find that outstretched hand
and change your destiny.
Reach for it,
to once again find the sun.
Reach for it,
to bring light to the dark that will lift you up and
inspire you -
so that you can find your way
back to the path that you need to lead,
for the life that you want to live.

Unkindness

Those words you spoke
sadly seem to be permanently etched in my mind.
The flames smoldering, yet still burning
deep within my heart.
As if run thru by a sharp and gleaming sword,
there is now a gaping hole thru my very soul,
making me feel hollow,
as the blood from your wounding words
slowly trickles,
down,
down,
down.
I must decide soon,
how to stop the bleeding.
Words can hurt.
Words can change the dynamics
and once said, cannot be taken back.
I close my eyes and remember happier times.
Grateful for all of our yesterdays,
but feeling so very empty today.
I know I was supposed to call,
but I cannot be there today -
don't know about tomorrow,
and no idea at all about next week.
Because try as I might,
I cannot seem to erase
those words you spoke,
from my mind.

Thirsty

Trying so hard to forget his mistakes -
feeling his regrets.
Playing the *if only* game,
over and over in his mind.
Sadly leaving him
with feelings of unforgiveness and unworthiness.
Too often consuming him,
and sending him into his personalized version of the
Twilight Zone.
Like a top spinning … spinning… spinning.
Then slowing, slowing, slowing,
until finally falling over,
onto the dry, dusty, desert of discontent.
Lying there parched,
but anticipating the familiar mirage to reappear -
that oasis of liquid libation to lap,
where he will drink, drink, drink yet again -
in his futile attempt
to quench,
the unending thirst within his soul.

Sometimes

Sometimes when I close my eyes,
I see myself as a child,
lying on the grass with the little white daisies growing in it,
down by the big sand pile at the school.
Staring up at that big blue sky, my whole life to live,
and dreaming of being a ballerina on Broadway.
Sometimes when I close my eyes,
l feel the pain of an emotionally abusive marriage.
I see the pain in my son's eyes, and remember that hollow
feeling inside.
Stress from the seemingly endless court battles.
The resolve of never giving in.
Finally victorious,
in securing peace, and escaping a dark life.
Sometimes when I close my eyes
I see my life as a movie in fast forward mode -
everything blurry and rushed .
Within a few seconds,
everything queued up to right now.
Feeling fuzzy -lost - disoriented - trying to catch my breath.
Wondering how did I get here and what direction do I go
now.
Sometimes when I close my eyes my inner voice calms me.
My spirituality lifts me from a dark place and brings me
peace.
I feel gratitude of living my life and all the lessons learned on
my path.
I feel exuberant and bask in the love of my family, but most
importantly …
Before I open my eyes,
My soul feels healed, knowing my journey has made a
difference in the lives of my sons.

Ghostland

Go away ghosts
get out of my head,
swirling about,
stirring up old thoughts,
re-opening old wounds,
fueling old fears.
Rattling the chains from my past.
Trying to wrap them like a choke collar around neck,
thinking you will drag me back there to all the pain and
misery.
I have grown far too weary of those dark, shadowy thoughts
from long ago.
I will not let you take me back there – ever.
Your moans and groans
will no longer deter me or break me.
I have learned your tricks and grown wiser.
You can no longer strip away my pride.
Go away ghosts,
get out of my head,
I am immune to your mind games now.
Fear no longer drives me or makes me run.
Thoughts you conjure no longer cripple or debilitate me.
Finally unshackled from your emotional chains,
I am free.

Give and Take

So you are finding out now
that it's not always *all* about you,
at least it's not if you are with me.
I can bend like a willow, yes I can,
but baby you have be limber and stretch
when it's your turn as well.
You can't or you won't … which is it?
The buzzer sounds -
your time is up.
How do you not understand by now,
that life is what you make it.
Sometimes you gotta give
in order to get.
Take, take, take,
works well for awhile -
it works until you hit that wall,
and find yourself alone.
Feeling alone,
even with you are with someone.
That empty,
hollow,
solitary feeling
that you just can't shake.
Sitting and wondering,
why it doesn't feel so right anymore.
It is your soul speaking to you,
telling you that you need to
learn to give,
and learn to love,
by freeing your heart.
Only thru selflessness, love, and compassion,
can you ever become whole.
Love cannot flourish

in a heart that is small and shallow.
Joy cannot thrive,
in a soul that is closed and dark -
for without love and joy,
life is truly meaningless indeed.

Party's Over

When it's over,
it's hard not to feel like a complete idiot,
when you know the proverbial writing on the wall
was there all the time -
but you just chose not to read it.
Thinking by hanging on just a little bit longer that,
Abracadabra - the magic will return.
Poof - the flames of passion will re-ignite.
Getting smacked between the paddles of delusion and denial,
like a ping pong ball.
Back and forth, again and again.
Still not reading those words until that final whack
that sends you flying to the floor.
All those high hopes you had –vanished.
Reality finally dawns that no rabbit is going to get pulled out
of the hat,
and not even a spark can be found in the stone cold embers,
of what was once a blazing fire.
Somehow, some way though,
after floating down a river of tears,
you re-evaluate and find your self-worth once again.
You find the strength and resolve to move on, always to
wonder
how in the hell were you were there for so long –
ultimately finding gratitude in the lesson taught,
and never looking back.

Sister, Sister, Sister

My three sisters,
they push me when I need a boost, and pick me up when I
fall down.
They help to keep me grounded - they are my support pack.
And it's a reciprocal thing, because that's what sisters do.
It feels like we have our own special club that no one else
can join,
just us four … and we are quite the variety pack of
personalities.
But the special thing is,
my sisters are also three of my best friends.
Of course it wasn't always this way,
because being the baby sister of four,
meant that three more women besides my mama,
could and would get *all* in my business,
all of the time.
Bossy, bossy, bossy.
Still, I really cannot imagine my life without any of them.
It is the times we share,
it is the people we love and the memories we make,
that enhance our lives and make us rich.
There are just no better best friends than your sisters,
and my fabulous three are indelibly engraved in my heart.

Meltdown

The invisible line in the sand had been drawn,
I knew it was there,
it was just that I couldn't stay on the other side this time.
Now, all I can do is tread the water
streaming from the seemingly never ending flow.
Water emanating from those blocks of ice,
the ice that has run
over, across,
and thru my heart for so long.
The same icebergs, which now effortlessly keep melting
by your presence in my life.
Where did you come from?
Sentenced by my self-imposed,
self-preservation prison mode,
my heart had been slowly, steadily, shrinking,
by serving time in its solitary confinement cell.
There had been too many years of merely existing.
Uneventful - rudimentary and robotic .
Going thru the motions,
day after day after day after day.
How did you change so much so soon?
Unconditional love,
can make the mundane exhilarating,
the predictable spontaneous,
the ordinary outstanding.
No strings.
No judgments
No time limits.
I know there are no guarantees.
I know there is a risk and yet …
I am powerless to stop myself from rolling the dice of
emotion.
Sometimes you just have to take the chance,

and hope that Lady Luck is the wind at your back,
and love makes you a winner.
Yes, I am now out on the limb,
but after all,
that's where all the fruit is.

Letting Go

Her body has grown weary,
her bones aching and tired,
her mind in need of serenity and peace.
Almost all the others
have crossed over to the other side,
leaving her here to mourn their loss.
Her unfinished business complete,
yet she resists the urge to just let it come.
Something in her soul
tells her it's not her time just yet -
a bit more to do before she can let go.
The legacy of her life – her children,
validates her life and sustains her.
Ever the Mama Bear,
she valiantly tries to ensure,
that when her time comes,
her love, devotion, and care will transcend,
and still be felt.
She has been my rock,
for as long as I can remember.
I wish for her,
that she can find endless amounts of joy,
and all the happiness her heart can hold.
I hope for her,
that in these coming days,
she will learn to embrace life without worry,
and finally find the contentment that her soul seeks,
by stepping out on faith,
and knowing all will be well.

Unpolished

The scent of fresh sea air,
and the sounds of waves crashing against the shore.
A rocky hillside, a cascading waterfall -
any of the many gifts of nature,
instantly instills serenity and tranquility into the senses of a
man, who finds beauty in the simple things.
It's not the flash and prestige he seeks in life -
it's finding time in a world overrun from technology,
to sit on a beach or wander aimlessly in the ocean's waves.
To listen to the boom, boom, boom from a thunderous
storm, and watch the lightening from a picture window in a
candlelit room.
A simple man with a heart of gold,
who finds balance from life's daily grind,
by the harmony he finds in nature.
He is a diamond in the rough.
He can watch the ocean waves for hours,
digging his toes deep into the sand
while anticipating the ocean mist to softly spray across his
face.
Mother Nature in all her glory sustains him,
and gives him a reason to breathe.
There is a yearning in his very soul,
to stare at the stars,
to swim in the sea,
to wantonly wallow in the sultry sun on a late summer
afternoon.
Not all gems are polished and shiny,
look beneath the surface …
and perhaps you will uncover a treasure.

Crown Jewels

So many goals I set for myself,
I did not ever reach.
So many places I wanted to travel to,
I have never gone.
Seems like just yesterday,
I was staring down into pairs of chocolate and root beer
brown eyes.
Eyes that seemed to be illuminated
from the soft glow of the Disney night light in the corner.
Eyes that seemed to look into my very soul,
innately knowing I was their mother who would love them
always.
All those late night and early mornings,
while the rest of our world was sleeping … silently rocking in
the glider.
Time seemed to stand still,
as songs by David Sanborn softly played,
and lulled them back to dream land.
Inhaling that freshly bathed baby smell.
Feeling their soft breath on my neck.
Feeling the warmth from holding them close.
Feeling their heartbeat in sync with mine.
My two jewels …
they validate my life.
Goals and destinations not met are forgotten,
because they give me reason to never give up.
They give me reason to live by example.
Now, when I gaze up into those chocolate and root beer
brown eyes,
I know without a doubt,
that no sacrifice,
no struggle,
no amount of money,

was ever too great.
My babies are now men -
but will always be the two jewels in my crown,
forever giving me wealth unimaginable,
because they are priceless.

See-Saw

Why is it,
that love can make your heart soar and send you flying -
flying so high you begin to wonder if you should duck,
so you don't hit your head on the moon?
Why is it,
that love can send you spiraling down a black hole,
free falling way, way down - picking up speed
and not knowing when or if you will ever hit bottom.
It's a see-saw thing,
up and down,
down and up.
The one who makes your heart soar,
will undoubtedly send you spiraling downward sometimes as
well.
But ...
 if he is the one fate has sent to cross your path,
the one who is truly meant just for you -
he will also reach out,
to pull you back from the free fall.
Which is when you will realize
that all those prior descents into darkness,
were merely lessons for your heart and for your mind.
In appreciation.
In compassion.
In patience.
In compromise.
For love is simply not enough.
It is that mutual feeling
of acceptance and respect
that you innately feel.
It is that chemistry coursing thru your veins,
making your skin hunger,
and your passion burn hot.

It may take a lifetime to find that special one,
the one meant for you,
the one you cannot imagine living without.
Remember the lessons learned from those dark descending
times, the times when there were no outreached arms
extended to save you when your paths do cross.
Experiencing the feeling of being fully appreciated
is one of many things in this life that is absolutely priceless.
If you cherish the time spent together,
if you embrace the intimacy,
if you delight in the devotion,
then at the end of your life's journey,
there will be no regrets,
but instead marvelous memories,
forever etched in your mind and filling your heart for all
eternity.

Always

I want,
to grow old with someone,
and still hold hands
even when we're 82.
I want,
to stay in love.
I want someone,
with whom words are not always necessary,
because his eyes say it all when he looks at me,
and makes me feel brand new.
I want,
his heart to race from the anticipation of returning back
home to me
after spending time apart.
I want to be able to feel and to one day say,
that even after all these years,
I am still his favorite woman,
and that he, is still my favorite man.
I want the flames of our passion to always burn hot,
and I especially want his arms to always be there
for the serenity and comfort,
that only his embrace can bring.
Hand in hand, heart to heart,
I want,
to stay in love.
Madly.
Passionately.
Deeply.
Always.

That Woman

I just may be,
the woman who your mother warned you about.
The elusive and mysterious woman who calls to you in your
dreams.
I will make your pulse race - and steal your breath away.
Passion is the trump card in my deck,
embrace the danger if you so dare.
I just may be,
that woman you won't wonder if you can live with,
but instead, know that you cannot live without.
That woman who you fall deliriously in love with,
all over again, everyday.
I just may be,
that woman who eases your mind, and soothes your soul.
The one who charms you and makes you smile,
even on your darkest of days,
then leads you to the radiant rainbow that shines after the
storm.
If I am that woman,
who glistens from the light of your soul, and steals your
heart, know that I will protect and treasure it always.
After a day of chasing dreams together,
as the sun sets and the night begins,
I will lay you down to sleep every night,
until the end of time.

Dreamscapes

Sometimes at night,
I sneak into your dreams,
so that we can be together.
Wild and spontaneous,
often travelling to exotic places.
Making passionate love,
under cascading tropical waterfalls,
or slow and tenderly on white sand beaches at sunset.
We dine alfresco,
 at a quaint little cafe in Paris.
Under the illuminating glow of a full moon,
we stroll hand in hand,
along the shimmering water of the Seine.
Warm summer nights in your backyard,
nestled and slowly rocking in a hammock,
we gaze in wonder at a star filled sky,
sharing hopes, wishes, and dreams for the days to come.
The things we do – the places we go
only matter because they are spent with you.
Perhaps some of my dreams might come true, someday.
But then again it doesn't really matter,
as long as I,
remain the one,
for whom your body hungers and your heart beats for.
As long as your arms are always there to hold me,
and your lips continue to crave mine …
then I want to be wherever you are.
The memories we make,
and the laughter we share,
will always, *always* -
make me count the moments and sneak into your dreams,
until we are together once again.

Night Love

Lying close in the still of night,
hearts beating in sync.
Music drifts thru the door from the forgotten stereo
still playing in the living room.
Barry White's voice speaking of love and passion,
fills the midnight air.
Light touches, soft caresses, our eyes closed
as the moon watches us thru the window.
My soul feels soothed and recharged.
The energy that fuels our desire sustains us -
words are not necessary.
Exhaling finally …
in the arms of the man
who freed me from my arctic prison,
and captured my heart.

Insatiable

The doorbell rings finally,
and my morning anticipation comes to an end ...
then begins all over again,
as I am enveloped in his arms.
His scent.
His touch.
His lips finding mine over and over again.
I am under his spell, and he under mine.
The heart pounding desire quickly building to a fever pitch.
Clothes discarded and strewn down the hallway,
as our passion takes control.
Lovin' so good it's almost abuse, as we lose ourselves,
over and over and over again.
Insatiable.
Sweat drenched.
Barely catching our breath as we make up for lost time.
Our bodies driving to their destination – ecstasy -
and we arrive there,
again and again and again.

Skin Hunger

My skin hungers
for his touch.
My body aches to feel,
his kisses,
his caresses,
his tongue.
I yearn to hear him
softly whisper in my ear
words of his passion for me.
He makes my pulse race from
the carnivorous craving,
and animalistic anticipation,
of feeling his body
beside me,
on top of me,
inside of me.
Completely enraptured,
he ignites my passion.
I overflow in anticipation,
of pleasures yet to come.

Late Dining

I hear the garage door close as I stir the spaghetti sauce.
Silent and stealth-like he walks in.
Though I can't see him,
I feel his presence behind me.
Instinctively I turn the gas off and put the spoon down.
Dinner will be late again.
Goosebumps pop up all over,
as I feel his hot breath moving closer and closer.
Standing in a state of anticipation,
until my body shudders,
as I feel that first electrifying kiss
on the nape of my neck.
His slow, seductive, stimulation,
tantalizing and teasing,
making me yearn for more.
My skin hungers for his touch.
Heart pounding,
Pressure rising.
Barely catching my breath.
He hungrily caresses my curves,
while whispering in my ear
of how good I smell -
always.
Skirt falling to the floor – blouse undone
underwear seems to disappear.
He kisses my lips and tells me they are sweet,
and taste of ripe strawberries.
I am weak.
The cold Mexican tile welcomes my body
as we fall to the floor.
Delicious desire driving our bodies.
Manic and mesmerized.
Ecstatic.

Exhilarated.
Euphoric.
A relentless excursion of ecstasy.
We ride high on the swelling waves of passion,
until finally ... we wipeout.
Our bodies spent and satiated,
we slowly drift in the ebbing tide,
carnally content, until we reach the shore again.

Breathless

My body belies my mind when I'm with him.
That incessant babble in my brain,
slowly begins fading away,
by the intoxicating sound of his voice.
My skin hungers for his touch,
and his for mine.
The energy that draws us together
ignites the flame of passion, that burns within us.
Hearts pounding, pulses racing.
Breathless - we are engulfed by desire.
Lips, tongues, touches.
Yearning.
Needing.
Wanting.
Overwhelmed - we surrender over and over,
until finally,
we can breathe again.

About the Author

Jamie Laster, has worked in the title industry for 27 years, but writing has always been her dream and her passion. By necessity she became a single mother, and has endured the trials and tribulations of single motherhood for over 18 years. Her spirituality and love of family, is what she attributes to bringing her through dark times and tragic circumstances throughout her life. She wrote *Life, Love & Passion: Reflections of My Soul*, to share her reflection, feelings and sentiment of those years.

A Message from Jamie

I hope you found something in my book that you could relate to, make you smile, or fuel your imagination.

If you could take a moment to leave me an honest review at Amazon, I'd really appreciate it.

Thank you for your support and reading my book!

Please visit my Web Site at JamieLasterAuthor.com.

www.ingramcontent.com/pod-product-compliance
Lightning Source LLC
Chambersburg PA
CBHW020444030426
42337CB00014B/1394